CW00407041

April 2020

Supported by

香港藝術發展局
Hong Kong Arts Development Council

Hong Kong Arts Development Council fully supports freedom of artistic expression. The views and opinions expressed in this project do not represent the stand of the Council.

The objectives of this book, *The Year of the Apparitions*, can be summed up in one word, survival. The survival game is hard for everyone. In my case, the stories that poetry and theatre can tell are life-vests fitting me amazingly well, painting was another one for a while. Stories not only help us to stay afloat, a good story is still the most powerful engine in the world, as it has been in the last few thousand years. My poems are short stories, open to interpretation, a little bit provocative, full of images. In this book I think I have managed to make my stories more solid. I believe that they are told in a way comprehensible to people from many backgrounds. We are all survivors.

José Manuel Sevilla was born in 1959 and has been publishing poetry since 1991. He has lived happily in Hong Kong since 2003 and has participated actively in artistic life. His series of photographs, "Street Language", was first exhibited at the Fringe Club in Ice House Street. He wrote poems for the ballet "Sombras, Sol y Flamenco", staged at the Sheung Wan Civic Centre in 2012. His play, "The Bridge" was performed at the McAuley Theatre, Hong Kong Arts Centre in 2011; another, "Kennedy", was performed in the same Theatre, in 2016. In 2012, his poem, 'Sonia Wants to Rent an Apartment', was awarded first prize in the *Cha* Encountering Poetry Contest, *Asian Cha* magazine. He was included in the poetry anthologies *Mingled Voices 2* and *Mingled Voices 3*, published in 2018 and 2019 respectively by Proverse Hong Kong.

The Year
of the
Apparitions

José Manuel Sevilla

Proverse Hong Kong

The Year of the Apparitions
by José Manuel Sevilla
First edition published in paperback in Hong Kong
by Proverse Hong Kong
Copyright © Proverse Hong Kong, April 2020.
ISBN: 978-988-8491-91-9

Distribution (Hong Kong and worldwide)
The Chinese University Press of Hong Kong,
The Chinese University of Hong Kong,
Shatin, New Territories, Hong Kong SAR.
Email: cup@cuhk.edu.hk; Web: www.cup.cuhk.edu.hk

Distribution (United Kingdom)
Stephen Inman, Worcester, UK.

Distribution and other enquiries to:
Proverse Hong Kong, P.O. Box 259, Tung Chung Post Office,
Lantau, NT, Hong Kong SAR, China.
Email: proverse@netvigator.com; Web: www.proversepublishing.com

The right of José Manuel Sevilla to be identified
as the author of this work
has been asserted by him in accordance with
the Copyright, Designs and Patents Act 1988.

Cover design by Artist Hong Kong.
Cover photo, "Little Fairy", Ma Wan, by José Manuel Sevilla.

British Library Cataloguing in Publication Data
A catalogue record is available
from the British Library

Prior Publication Acknowledgements

The four-poem sequence, "Of Words and Keys", was first published in *Mingled Voices 3: International Proverse Poetry Prize Anthology 2018*, Proverse Hong Kong, 2019.

The Year
of the
Apparitions

José Manuel Sevilla

Dedicated to

The heroes of Catalonia and Hong Kong

THE YEAR OF THE APPARITIONS

José Manuel Sevilla

Table of Contents

Prior Publication Acknowledgements   5
Author's Introduction   13

Pilgrim   17
I only live to give happy ends away   19
Indians   21
The Talking Photo   23
The Thief of Baghdad   26

Of Words And Keys
Memory, Future and Everyday Lies
Voices in my head   31
Silence is not sad   33
Soul Cleaning   35
Keys   37

The best day of our life   39
The Year of the Apparitions   40

Notes   59
Advance responses to José Manuel   61
Sevilla's *The Year of the Apparitions*

Introduction

Spain is probably the biggest disappointment of my life. Somebody said of that country that it was like a bad mother. I find it true, she never loved me, I never loved her. My good real mother arrived in Barcelona as a young Spanish immigrant woman running away from centuries of misery and gave me life in a beautiful and civilized small country by the blue sea called Catalonia.

Spain now is a bad apparition. Bad apparitions are its leaders, its history, many of its fierce people. However, many Spaniards and many Spanish things have shaped me: the bread, the bars, the smell of the world under the sun, Madrid, Segovia, Quevedo, the Second Republic, García Lorca, Don Juan Tenorio, Galdós, Machado, Javier Marías, Millás, Atraco a las 3, Almodóvar, Paco Ibáñez, la Mala Rodríguez, las Folías, Picasso, the redeeming cartoons of Forges, the photos of García-Alix and García-Rodero, Torrente, a book from Luisa Castro, a poem by Antonio Colinas, the language... The best me is written in Spanish, the angry me comes from Spain.

Living is an incessant flow of apparitions. Beings from other worlds entering ours, whom we decide to ignore, accept, fight, follow or believe to be out of our reach. They are not angels. You, the Reader are not an angel either, nor am I.

On 28th February 1994, Julie made her first apparition in my life on a plane flying from Barcelona to Athens. Since then, she has been appearing daily in one way or another. From that day, all changed for good: our son Alvaro, Hong Kong, the traveling, the views from our homes, the learning from each other to survive laughing and loving and drinking, the endless doses of future.

I wonder what I was for Julie before that plane to Athens, certainly not nothing because I was the future. Were there hints of me? Was I being expected? Desired? Is that a way of being? And being what?

What about family? As apparitions when we join a family, we are necessarily accepted. In the absence of freedom, consequences can be terrible. Actually, they are. The past is powerful in the family. The future is strong when we appear to strangers with a loving heart. This interests me deeply and pushes poetry out of me.

I find that the apparition of a delicate, vulnerable but determined alien being taking you into a different world and carrying you wherever worlds go is beyond marvelous, almost absurd, almost tragic. Poetic.

José Manuel Sevilla
Hong Kong, April 2019

Pilgrim

Going on holidays on a wagon out of control
chased by howling Indians painted for war
was a debatable idea.
Although I had my licence
we suffered an accident
and my head went flying out.
My body stayed sitting on the wagon
next to a pregnant Handmaid of Gilead,
with the reins in one hand and the mobile in the other.
We looked like one of the pictures
that my ex-wife had cut out
or a vandalized living crèche,
I always wanted to be part of one
to be photographed by strangers,
my indecency was not young and distracted.

After that came the Surgery of the Century,
the sewing of my head,
the first distant noises,
the party of the medical team,
the eyes opening and
the anaesthetist vomiting by the hospital equipment,
the months with images passing by
like underground stations on a train without breaks.

I remember the sea full of plastic carnations,
the corrupt on the beach with their families,
the rotten apple speaking in a dark-coloured language
and the others quiet and listening
and rapidly changing their colour,

I remember a part of the map
where kings and subjects alike
prayed to heaven
but loved the sewers for not being seen from it.

José Manuel Sevilla: The Year of the Apparitions   17

I remember a piece of the starred sky
falling down on a flag like a blessing,

I remember being an apple and not being quiet
and being bitten and swallowed
and I remember sleeping and dreaming in a big stomach.

And then the hospital again
and a lady surgeon vomiting by the equipment
and my wedding with her
and I vomiting without her
and one day I leave the cat in charge
and take a taxi to the border of nowhere
and start my pilgrimage to the middle of nowhere
which is my present life and probably the next.

I am a jellyfish in a sea full of plastic carnations
but I always believed in the generosity
of the winds.

I only live to give happy ends away

When the last circus shut the door,
the very few Knife-Throwers alive
—who had struggled and suffered so much—
rounded me up out of their wits
speaking to me all at the same time,
red as beetroots.
I didn't belong to the trade union,
I was not their lawyer,
I was just a happy ends writer,
what could someone like me possibly do for them?

I told them that this world was a war
and that in a war whether you had the floor under your feet
or not
was at the beginning or at the end of it,
in between it was like a picnic,
fight, pain but mere routine.
Aye.

The repeats of life, the Death visits,
the weekends flat broke, the beatings,
the next door screams of husbands to wives and of wives to
husbands,
what else could they remember?
Aye.

But I myself put my memories in the happy endings I write,
like the boy on a Barcelona roof
watching the sunny sheets hung up in the wind
ripping off from their body their bad nights.
Aye.

Well, that was it, pals. Finito.
Oh, no, here we go again.

When I finally shouted them up,
I told them about the Southern Hemisphere stars.
None of the characters in my short tales had seen them
but they always wondered
—and I couldn't do anything about it—
the Southern Hemisphere stars,
for whom would they be twinkling?

At the end, if I always managed to write them a happy end,
the Knife-Throwers had to think in those same terms,
at the end of the day, they were loaded with knives.

Where had they left their assistants? I asked.
For God's sake, what happened to their smiling Knife-
Thrower Assistants?
And to their legs? To what kind of public are they showing
them now?
The hundreds of lights that sparkled on their skins
for whom were they shining now?

And then the last legitimate Knife-Throwers alive,
raised their eyes to the sky.
And so did I.

We had never seen anything more beautiful,
the Southern Hemisphere stars slightly trembling
but resilient,
holding their breath
but smiling,
waiting for the arrival of the next knife.

Indians

When I was a kid the Indians killed me
on my parents bed in a thousand different manners.
Time does not fear anything
but facing a plastic gun it runs away like a coward.
You are a kid while the Indians chase and corner you,
until one day the Comanche get an order
and they suddenly retire while their howling
fades in the distance.

The first quiet day of my life
it was announced that the traditional eternity was not
sustainable any more
and the four hundred plus living gods passed by a wide
margin
the definitive closing down of Hell.
All the excitement, gone.
Time grabbed my neck from the back
and thus my childhood ended.

At the beginning, I dedicated myself to small thefts in book
stores.
When I decided to return all the books, they caught me.
Since then I hate irony, specially that of destiny.

HVS, Hooligan Voluntary Service, in residences for the
old:
at one time that was the fashion.
Secret mischiefs in the shelter were cooler than
fighting with the light-sabre against the air in your room.
Furthermore, if class is what you do when nobody is
looking,
cruelty in private has always been a sign of nobility.

Then, game over. What happened afterwards is a different
story.

Now I am an angel,
like everybody else,
only the alcohol has atrophied my wings.
I don't have money for the arrows
and with the excuse of tattooing the compulsory arrowed
heart,
they anaesthetised me and removed my sex.

What else can I say?
No War-painted Indians.
Nights are long.
Don't come.

The Talking Photo

Aunty Trinidad tells,
that soon after she arrived in heaven,
an angel that back on Earth had been a little bit a con artist
and a little bit her brother-in-law,
showed up with a trumpet for annunciations
and a blackboard because he couldn't speak.
His voice in this world was prisoner in a very strange
and captive way.

Aunty, who knew the ways of life,
laughed for the first time after her funeral
and fed up of the blackboard, said to him that
only the Sun, the Moon and the vehemence
—that's how she called the pushes of sex—
come back to the world
and that she would believe otherwise only
when the son comes back to the mother's belly
or the statue of Don Juan in Seville
comes back to the lost wax.

My voice didn't die, it stayed in a photo,
wrote the angel,
and that photo is on Earth, that's why I come to you, Trini,
I've waited so long for you.

And then it all changed.

Aunty Trinidad remembered,
with an unaccustomed shock,
that I had a talking photo.
Sometimes talking a lot,
sometimes quiet for weeks.
I have it in the living room,
inside a frame from El Corte Inglés,
in front of the TV and next to a phone

José Manuel Sevilla: The Year of the Apparitions   23

(where a vengeance
that is not relevant now,
was born),
some bottles of smells of the middle class and
my albums with all the family lies.

Very few know about the talking photo—
I never receive visits at home
and Mrs Raquel, who does not fear the dead
but the followers of Mr Trump,
cleans it with a bit of bad mood   three times a week
quiet or talking—

I have heard that voice, from someone
behind the camera
that took the photograph of my parents
on their wedding day,
hundreds, thousands of times.

My beliefs guide me without excess
and always welcome me
when I look at the watch, stopped at 8.15
in Hiroshima;
or when I take a bath in the waters
where the African immigrants sink;
or when the shame of being born in a country of thieves
        burns.

These are my secrets.
The things that accompany me also have secrets:
the switched off TV with the Twin Towers inside,
the phone, the bottles, the albums.

And the photo where a hidden man whispers

    "It's done. Tonight, at nine."

José Manuel Sevilla: The Year of the Apparitions   24

Finally I know whose is the voice of the talking photo.
What I don't know is who listened and why it mattered.
She will never tell me,
Aunty Trinidad.

The Thief of Baghdad

The kids grew up,
they spoke of life and death
as if they had been there,
they smoked their cigarettes,
and walked to their cars.

Their world, those crazy heartbeats,
where was it?
In the motorway?

You are all the same there,
you all go at the speed of light
to the same place
and one cannot spot the pure heart
among the many bad of you anymore.
That's what I told them
and it is known
that words once said don't come back like a dog
when you whistle.
They extinguished their cigarettes
and loudly closed the car doors.
They flew away, their cars screeching
desperately looking for the way in.

Look at me. Alone. Not liked. Saying those things.
I used to have small hands drawing
coloured boats with their black smoke.
I had to find them.
I had one wish left.

I was a thief in Baghdad
and a guide dog of a blind prince in Spain,
I had learnt to recognise
which were the eyes of a broken love
from the eyes that see the prey
for him.

He had taught me that strangers dress themselves up,
get close to you and put sugar in their voice
but we never really know what they will do with their
hands.
Some time later, a genie on a beach
granted me three wishes.

I was not a dog anymore,
many strangers dressed themselves up and came closer to
me.
That was long ago.
Today I have put my last things in the hands of somebody
that looked like the dog of a poor prince.
I was looking at my face on the glass
of a ticketing box office
when somebody tapped my shoulder.
Excuse me, are you done?

Almost, Sir. I was granted three wishes
of which I have only one left.
When I was young I had a return ticket
but it fell down my heart
and the things that had never found their way out
devoured it instantly.
This is my last wish, Sir, a new return ticket.
Today is not any day to me
and I thank you for your patience,
you surely know that the words once said
do not come back like a dog
when you whistle.

OF WORDS AND KEYS
Memory, Future and Everyday Lies

Voices in my head

I had a grandma
who first was a nun
and then lived in a cave.
I think I know that, at some point
between these two things,
she started to say—because she believed it—
that you do not bargain with the heart.
Or to believe it because she said it.
Hearts pump,
they push and push
up to the tip of your hands,
until they wake them up, naked like keys;
but you do not ask them what they open, what they close.
It's better to leave them counting,
the hands;
that's why they have fingers.
The ass has other things,
but don't ask it to count your money,
that's what my grandma used to say—
or maybe never said but I heard it—
you do not bargain with the voices in your head.

Why didn't you come to the funeral
I would not do this to my worst enemy
Give me back the keys
I can't marry you
Why did you tell him
Why didn't you tell him
I swear it was
I swear it wasn't
You were a son of a bitch.
You are a son of a bitch.

I had a grandma
who first was a nun
and then lived in a cave.
I know that, at some point
between these two things,
she was a refugee,
I was told
I wasn't told
Give me back the keys
Why didn't you come to the funeral.

Silence is not sad

Silence is not sad.
Silent movies are.
A bed is also sad.
That's why I was not born on a bed:
my mother gave birth to me standing up, alone,
gripping a window
and holding me with her legs.
Legs are not sad,
not those of a woman.

The army is sad.
There they didn't teach me how to drink,
of that I knew a fucking lot.
But I learned how to sleep on the floor,
march, slip away with the gipsy girls, all that;
not much, what military life back then could give.
Writing letters.
I got a postcard from my cousin Belen,
the one with a glass eye.
She killed herself in a motorbike accident.
The postcard was all black of course, no words.
When you die you become illiterate again.
Imagine, to go back to study all those school books,
with the drawing of the devil speaking at your ear;
so easy to become a sinner.
One of our neighbours in Jerusalem Street was a sinner—as
if taken out from our books, shorter though—he only
smoked when playing the piano
and his wife was a drunk;
those two were not friends with words;
losing a war didn't favour them too much.

I had lost it too, but that was long before I was born.
It's a long silent movie
before somebody gives birth to you.

Soul Cleaning

They found not much, the thieves
who burgled our future:
some friendship in cash, a few hopes
that my mother had left me;
but all the words were in a mess—
everything we were supposed to say,
in the years to come,
scrambled on the floor, on the bed, in the kitchen,
the sentences in our wardrobes thrown everywhere,
as if a typhoon had passed.

In the kids' room we found
my elder daughter's only prayer to the Lord:
"I follow this diet with joy,
I am a lighter burden to You,"
next to the Walter White quote
that we kept in the safe—
it's not a grandmother's jewel,
but it has sentimental value
and it's been so useful to me—
"There must exist certain words in a specific order
that could explain all of this,
but I just can't ever seem to find them".

All over the place were the bad words,
the moans, the screams—
I like them; bad as they are, they also clean,
as, in the old times, heretics were forced
to swallow red-hot iron, in what was called
Soul Cleaning.

How wrong have people always been, wanting
to go to heaven.

When I stumbled into, "Rome does not pay traitors",
I looked around once more.
What did the burglars really expect to find
in our future?
Rome always pays traitors.

Keys

The man who killed me came zigzagging
in the big truck through Rage Street.
It was my turn.
Shit, this life gets pregnant with unwanted pregnancies
every other day—well, that's why, in our family,
we all carried our keys
to the Kingdom of Heaven
with us, all the time.
You never know.

At home they made us fear many things—
like bathing before two hours after we accepted candies
from strangers—
But, losing those keys!
We could lose friendship, direction, time, the match, hope,
the north, faith, virginity, memory, shame, respect, temper,
even lose reflection in the mirror
and feed only on blood.
But not the damned keys.

Luckily, it was already Sunday morning.
During the years I lived with my family,
Sundays at 9 o'clock was the time to open the windows and
let the smell of fish go;
and at 10, to let the words that were like arrows go;
when, after the rice and siesta, it was time to learn
how to make snowmen;
because you never know.

I used to think with nostalgia of the wolves
who raised me,
of how today we would enjoy learning
all this unknown wickedness
coming from Saudi Arabia and the USA;
but my mother was quite strict;
she had not left her house to drag me along out of the
jungle, still wearing her apron,
to, you know.

I almost don't smell of a living man anymore,
the lines on my hands are like last month's newspaper.

It's about time to stop floating
on my back with the others,
as if Rage Street was a crowded swimming pool,
and grab the bag of El Corte Inglés
in which I have my tunic,
for the opening of the Red Sea,
because, you never know.

But what really nobody knows
is
that I also have a hidden set of keys
to the Kingdom of Wolves.

My heart still lives in the jungle,
believing that the war is not over.

The best day of our life

Again we filled up an apartment,
again stepped on new sidewalks
quiet like horses that we would have to tame.

Again we began, stubborn, insolent
like people being born,
we let the dogs of the neighbourhood smell us,
taking for a walk those unleashed godless souls of ours,
we surely had to negotiate.

Here the flowers told us
of a promised land that wasn't this one,
they all talk about the same, always, everywhere,
but we liked their accent that we didn't know.

No word in our mouths
stood up to let the name of this day have a seat,
damned words gossiping bad news
like 20th century televisions,
playing cards and throwing ash on the tongue.
We saw a beautiful fountain
for humans and dogs
and we rinsed our mouths,
it was the best day of our life.

It was the best day of our life,
from that day we would listen to
all our hearts every night
the ears close to the chest,
we heard them stubborn, insolent
beating over the siren of a distant ambulance
only then we could sleep.

The Year of the Apparitions

Mr. January, the very honourable, if I may.

You appeared in my wardrobe
far from the light and the commotion.
I love to feel trapped among your ladies' dresses,
he told me,
they smell of parties.
He also told me, Do not say I am an angel,
Don't even dare.

After death there is no sex but
there are minted cigarettes.
After that first revelation from Mr. January,
I looked for the dead Camel
that I had hidden in my home.
I confess I am the serial killer
of the good old times.
I think I am wanted.

Mr. January went on, unchanging, saying
that smoking the same thing on both sides
was like the French language between France and Belgium
or the Dutch language between Belgium and Holland;
I prefer to say nothing about the jokes that followed.

In his second revelation, he told me
that heaven was an abandoned mining town,
gold ran out a long time ago, Sevilla, don't try to go there,
etcetera.

His third revelation was an omen:
after the atomic bomb the world's soul is a desert of sand;
you will cross the desert
where you will find a door; you will open it and
the world will take you on its shoulders

wherever worlds go.

He chalked up a white M
on my back:
The good old times are looking for you
you will be accountable but don't worry,
they are like the Camels you believed were dead.
Carry a lighter with you,
you will know what to do when the time comes.
And he left leaving a cloud of tobacco behind him.
Minted.

…

Mr. February, the very honourable, if I may.

You appeared in my wardrobe
far from the light and the commotion.
I love to feel trapped among your ladies' dresses,
he told me,
they smell of parties.
He rejected being called an angel.

He described death as a house
with doors void of possibilities
and windows with views to be forgotten.
I asked him if heaven was an abandoned mining town
and he answered that it was something worse:
heaven was a mirror.

He smoked like a chimney
which did not prevent him from stealing
anything within reach.
After his visit I missed
some characters from my books,
like King Macbeth, from Scotland.

Refined by nature, he praised the virtues
of life accepted as a summer souvenir,
without clouds and temperature;
and he asked me about my future.
Mounting my white horse and before riding away
with the music of The Virginian, I shouted,
Mr. February,
the world will take me on its shoulders
wherever worlds go.

…

Mr. March, the very honourable, if I may.

You appeared in my wardrobe
far from the light and the commotion.
I love to feel trapped among your ladies' dresses,
he told me,
they smell of parties.
He rejected being called an angel, like the rest.

Of course there is a light after death,
my good man!
He clicked his tongue, inhaled the cigarette, let the smoke
go
and went on like this:
Flash news, my innocent friend: marketing!
Who can possibly get lost once they're dead?
The light and all that… marketing. Do you get it,
Sevilla?
Google Maps is just a leak from the other world,
like many others.
I begged him for some examples,
after that
I stopped my non-taxable donations.

I asked him if heaven was a mirror and, letting out a loud laugh,
he answered that it was something much worse.
The mirror is this,
you dumbass,
and then,
More flash news, Sevilla: gin mixed with tonic
in the same glass, isn't it clever?

I didn't overlook the my good man thing
and I kindly asked him if that was for real
but from his sort of superior position
he reproached me my days,
leaving like birds or clouds running somewhere,
I'm not sure.

Finally, making peace, he asked about my future.
Smoking and sitting on a bench
not seeing the ravens gathering behind me
I told him,
the world will take me on its shoulders
wherever worlds go.

…

Mrs. April, the very honourable, if I may.

You appeared in my wardrobe
far from the light and the commotion.
I love to feel trapped among your men's suits,
she told me,
they smell of parties.
She rejected being called an angel, like the rest.

The Garden of Eden still resists.
Adam and Eve are still alive and naked, she told me,
and she gave me a leaf of the Tree of the Knowledge of

Good and Evil.
We smoked and drank. Gin&Tonics. She crossed her legs
and I watched them.
When she touched up her lips
I asked her,
If this is heaven's mirror, then God is you?
She stood up and smacked the crap out of me,
saying,
You are such a dumb-ass, Sevilla,
heaven is much worse than that.
In heaven, or in what's left of it,
there's nothing else than religion.

Sunk into despair,
I snatched the black telephone from Ana Magnani
and told Mrs. April that the world will take me on its
shoulders
wherever worlds go.
And she on the other end of the line,
whispered with her minted-breath
Don't you ever save yourself.

…

Mrs. May, the very honourable, if I may.

You appeared in my wardrobe
far from the light and the commotion.
I love to feel trapped among your men's suits,
she told me,
they smell of parties.
She rejected being called an angel, like the rest.

Many nights like this, she told me,
I stayed in my bed, motionless,
breathless, hoping that the tiger of life
passed by not seeing me one more day.

This is what you get if you live enough
to see your mistakes knocking at your door,
grown up and ready to stay.
If you knew how much pleasure
this body gave me
and many others that sometimes had a name,
sometimes didn't.

Mrs. May lit another cigarette and told me,
In your dreams there is a rumour about
orgies, dunes, something about a tiger...
She exhaled a cloud of minted smoke
and I fell asleep.

I dreamt that the naked back of the world was a desert.
There was a tiger getting closer,
there was a door behind me
in the middle of the sand
and someone was knocking.
I opened and saw some silhouettes
under the blinding light of the sun.
Who were they and what were they doing naked in my
bed?
When I wanted to ask their names
something squeezed my throat,
I don't know if a tiger's claw
or a storm of minted cigarettes.
I fell rolling down a dune.
There was a black telephone off the hook,
crying and begging in Italian.
The sand tasted like the atomic bomb.

...

Mr. June, the very honourable, if I may.

You appeared in my wardrobe

far from the light and the commotion.
I love to feel trapped among your ladies' dresses,
he told me,
they smell of parties.
He rejected being called an angel, like the rest.

Mr. June and I had an encounter
with some sudden intimacy
that had led us nowhere though.
It happened in a theatre when I stood up to let him go
to a seat further down on my right in the same row.
He would lose his head in a different encounter
from which his long relationship with the Afterlife
was born.
But I lost mine in the theatre.

In his first apparition, Mr. June took me
to a hotel downtown.
He undressed me delicately and put me to bed.
He closed my eyes with his hand
and I started to see the dreams
of all those that had slept in that room before.
I walked through them unseen,
I opened a door and entered the following dream.
When I woke up I felt like on a Monday before school.

I was lighting up a Camel sitting on the sheets,
when I realized that Mr. June
had left with my clothes, my wallet and
the scar on my thigh that had saved me
in many embarrassingly silent situations.
Thank God, there were green curtains in the room.

Mr. June in fact doesn't love
to be trapped in my wardrobe among my woman's clothing.
And light and commotion are to him like the air we breathe.
He doesn't take me to downtown hotels anymore

but to hostels near the train station.
We go to bed together
and he watches how I am being stripped of my humanity
in the dreams of others
again and again.
But when I wake up,
fallen and abandoned by everybody,
I slowly get up, raising my fist,
and God is my witness that I will never be hungry again,
and the world at last takes me wearing my green dress on
its shoulders
wherever worlds go.

…

INTERMISSION

…

Mr. July, the very honourable, if I may.

You appeared in my wardrobe
far from the light and the commotion.
I love to feel trapped among your ladies dresses,
he told me,
they smell of parties.

Don't call me an angel, Sevilla, not me, not anybody
because nobody is.
There was an adoption agency in the seventies
in South America, he told me,
that shaved chimpanzees
and sold them as human babies.
There was no internet back then,
I don't know how they managed.
They died forgotten
one after the other, once they finished their sentences,

two women and two or three men.
Well, they are together again,
as if death had nothing to do with them.
What for, nobody really knows,
the Afterlife is more complicated than you people think.

Mr. July had a theory.
The countries, Sevilla, exist because they already exist
when people are born.
Each head is a country,
many have walls, most of them are at war;
in some it's cold and in others there is not a single straight
street.
In my country, he said, there were legal murders
and illegal murders;
it depended on the quantity of spilled blood.
Despite that, I married twice,
had three sons and two granddaughters.
People actually like to go touring around
the nice sightseeing, and to go back home with some
souvenirs.
Back in their country. In their heads.

I invited Mr. July to the desert that lived in my dreams.
The dunes, the door in the middle of the sand.
When we opened it,
we saw a soundless documentary in black and white
of a happy white, western family
eating from cans in a fallout shelter.
My father was wearing a tie,
my sister was combing a doll's hair,
and I was writing my homework
under the attentive eyes of my mother.
You were an angel, Sevilla, Mr. July told me,
drunk,
pointing his revolver at me.
He turned around

and left laughing outloud like Liberty Valance.
He didn't see me,
slipping away from the shelter.

…

Mrs. August, the very honourable, if I may.

You appeared in my wardrobe
far from the light and the commotion.
I love to feel trapped among your men's suits,
she told me,
they smell of parties

I live in a post card,
she told me,
I am slim and I am the tourist with a big hat,
sunglasses, and a red bikini, next to a donkey loaded with
pots.
No burglar will sneak into my heart again
nor will get me pregnant again,
and above everything, no more words
will get close to my nose smelling like the fall of Rome.
What were you saying about the angels, sweetheart?

She said something else but I was not listening.
A plane passed and I stopped to look up at it,
a boy holding hands with his mother
also stopped.
When I looked down,
above the boy's head was the word 'Helsinki',
and above his mother's 'Stuttgart',
and above the head of a man carrying a backpack 'SW-
Funk',
and above the heads of everyone around me
were the beautiful names of the dials
of my childhood's radios,

José Manuel Sevilla: The Year of the Apparitions   49

Berlin W., RIAS, Vatican, Rome, Bruxelles 1, Praha,
Andorra, Porto 1, Madrid, Buenos Aires, Monte Carlo,
Rabat.
Thousands of voices from the radio flooded the air,
we had seen Nimrod
silver and shiny flying victorious in the sky,
higher than the tower he built to defy God
in Babylon.
Mrs. August had disappeared.

…

Mr. September, the very honourable, if I may.

You appeared in my wardrobe
far from the light and the commotion.

I only wanted to continue doing
what I used to do alive,
to work with my garbage truck
and my garbage workmates.
After work we used to drink champagne,
like the high and mighty,
every morning after a whole night
emptying bins and throwing bags into the truck.
I don't know, there was something magnificent
in cleaning the streets, like creating a new world.
I tried the cunts and then the family
but, you know what? there was a lot of garbage there too
and nobody cleaned it
and every day it piled up and no matter how many times
you showered, you smelled of trash big time.
However, now… don't die, friend, this is a big
boring shit.
In this death place there's no trash and
they don't need no fucking truck to collect it
and I miss the boys and the champagne

and the laughs,
we laughed so much that we forgot
to go to our weddings or to vote.
We drank more champagne than the rich.
That was the life.

Mrs. August had left me an old post card
of a beach with a small boat
and her, slim and smiling next to a donkey loaded with pots.
I gave it to Mr. September.

…

Mr. October, the very honourable, if I may.

A young teenager appeared in my wardrobe
far from the light and the commotion.
Bewildered, speechless, wide-eyed.
Nobody would take him for an angel.
Was he one of the first?
What did they do, the first to arrive?
Did they paint their hands on the walls of a cave?
Did they build pyramids or the Empire State?
Did they navigate and give away small mirrors to the
indigenous?
And the ones arriving today,
do they walk in the Afterlife looking at their mobiles?
Etcetera.

I offered him a cigarette that he rejected with a disgusted
look.
He didn't seem to know how to read.
I showed him a guitar and I spoke about Victor Jara,
about how they cut off his hands at the Santiago Stadium,
about the Argentinian prisoners that were pushed
from airplanes to their death in the sea,
about the babies that were stolen from the jailed pregnant

women,
about the killers of Garcia Lorca,
about their sons,
about their grandsons and granddaughters,

about the Rulers,

The Insignificant,
the Insensitive,
the Merciful with the Corrupt,
the Not-chosen,
the Diabolical,
the War,
the Dispenser of Anxiety,
the Distracted,
the Weak,
the Dominated,
the Negligible,
the Destructive,
the Terminator of Democracy,
the Deformer,
the Unforgiving
the Defeated at Decency,
the Miser,
the Hoarder,
the Opener of hearts to the Inquisition,
the Ignorant,
the Wasteful,
the Standoffish,
the Arrogant,
the Praise of the Backwards,
the Awarder of Exile,
the Humiliation of the Good,
the Omniscient of Curses,
the Psychic of the Repression,
the Judge and Jury,
the Unfair,

the Crude,
the Well informed by the Defamatory,
the Revenge,
the Small,
the Giver of Blame,
the Traitor,
the Infernal,
the Vitriolic,
the Nobody,
the Partner of the Wicked,
the Confounded,
the Clueless,
the Odious,
the Illegitimate,
the Resurrection of his vile progenitors,
the Lie,
the Shelter of the Bad,
the Protégé,
the Atrocious,
the Shrewd,
the Origin of the Loot,
the Restorer of the Criminals,
the Giver of life to the Old,
the Taker of life of the Ribbon Republic.

Etcetera.

He did not understand any of my words.
He fell asleep.
I saw him dreaming in my desert,
his naked body full of promise
like a map before the journey,
running towards the door in the middle of the sand.
He opened it and
a hurricane of light
swept the long horse of Death
riding over cities and countries,

the brutal hordes of the Rulers turned into ashes
like Nosferatu under the radiant light of the Sun,
and all the letters of the alphabet unanimously
voted to never form again the words

Motherland,
Empire,
Genocide,
Army,
Sharia,
Shooting,
Mutawa,
Apartheid,
Border,
Forbid,
Haram,
Macho,
Rape,
Fake,
Hate,
Race,
Wall,
Coup,
Post-truth,

Etcetera.

Amen.

…

Mrs. November, the very honourable, if I may.

You appeared in my dream
in a street of Mexico City called Enchanted,
your soul looked to me like a silence
detached from the voices and commotion of people,

as if you had been let go from the sea when it ends on the sand.

You looked at me as mirrors do,
to show me the under-eye bags growing
after the farce of the judiciary,
the wrinkles in my forehead deeper
every time I hear my national anthem,
how fantasies desert,
the expulsion of the truth from our lives,
the dog that runs after our car while we are moving away,
the fall of the flesh under the weight of darkness.

Ashes started to rain
and the planes over the Palacio de la Moneda were heard,
and the tanks in Prague,
and in a bus Spanish policemen shouted After them!
happy as if they were going to a football match
with their hearts pumping blood and promises
like a map before the journey.

I was in Poland while the ashes rained from the sky,
Mrs. November said to me breaking the silence,
I was in Prague inside that tank,
I was in Mexico City,
I was in Santiago
that one in black and white is me
leading to death those with the hands up,
I was in Sarajevo,
I was in Raqqa,
I was in Charlottesville,
I was in Barcelona and I went after them.

Goodbye Mrs. November,
your heart is a map after the journey.

…

Mrs December, the very honourable, if I may.

Probably you mistook the door,
but you breathed my wardrobe;
and I saw you when your heart began to pump the desire
from the lungs to your head, the legs, the belly, the hands,
the breasts.

She tasted of mint
Mrs. December.
Perhaps she had a disease still hiding
or perhaps it was an imprisoned truth.
Perhaps some news was going to meet her,
this never can be known,
this I couldn't know
when she was whispering at my ear,
Call me angel,
I'm your angel,
she let me smell inside her body,
Mrs. December,
and she let me look at her forbidden places
when I saw it tattooed on her skin,
the most hated sign in the world.

She had her eyes closed
Mrs. December
because she did not care
if I could hear, smell, see.
But I saw it
and I couldn't not see it.
My fingers hurt
when I touched her,
and then the hands and the belly and the sex and the legs
and the head and my heart pumped
the pain into my lungs.
I stopped hearing
and smelling

and seeing
and it hurt what I touched and what I didn't touch,
I stopped feeling my dimly-lit room,
the temperature went away.

The screams arrived bit by bit,
the time seconds knew,
they had heard them before,
all the screams,
every second recognized them
that's why they didn't pause
and passed me by
like a train
illuminated in the night.

I was back in the desert.
There was a tiger getting closer,
there was a door behind me
in the middle of the sand
and someone was knocking.
I opened and saw some silhouettes
under the blinding light of the sun.
Who were they and what were they doing naked in my
bed?
When I wanted to ask their names
they looked at me for an instant,
they smiled and carried on their orgy
on Mrs. December.
She had her eyes open
and looked at me,
her mouth was open
and smiling
muttered my name,
then she ignored me
and abandoned herself to her desire.

I turned around,

opened the door
and I appeared in my wardrobe
far from the light and the commotion.
I felt trapped among my ladies' dresses
and my men's suits.
They smelled of parties.

NOTES ON THE POEMS

'Silence is not sad'

José Manuel Sevilla has explained some of the background to his poem, 'Silence is not sad', as follows: "The Catholic Religion was compulsory in schools in Franco's Spain. The books for Primary school students were full of cartoons. The image of a boy free of sin was always of a fair-haired, clean young man with stainless clothes—you could smell his mummy's eau-de-cologne on him. An Aryan. The image of a sinner was of a dirty, angry-faced and rather tall boy with, messy brown hair. He was dark-skinned. Obviously."

'Soul Cleaning'

Asked to explain to readers who the "Walter White" referred to in his poem, 'Soul Cleaning', is, José Manuel Sevilla writes: "Walter White—also known by his clandestine pseudonym "Heisenberg"—is the leading character in the multi-awarded American TV series *Breaking Bad*, played by Bryan Cranston. Mr. White is a talented chemist and a teacher who spends his life in a grey position in a secondary school. A loving family man, he is diagnosed with terminal lung cancer. To save his family financially, he goes into partnership with one of his pupils—a minor street dealer—to produce the best quality methamphetamine, which he is able to do thanks to his knowledge of Chemistry. An amazing resurrection, in Albuquerque, of Dr Jekyll and Mr Hyde."

José Manuel Sevilla explains that, "Rome does not pay traitors", is a common saying in Spanish. "Legend says that the Romans had to fight a pro-independence movement in Hispania. Consul Scipio plotted with three of its members, close to the rebel leader, Viriathus, to betray and kill him. When the three came to claim their reward, Scipio replied, 'Rome does not pay traitors', prioritising ethics over the fact that their action had been initiated by him."

ADVANCE RESPONSES
to JOSE MANUEL SEVILLA'S,
THE YEAR OF THE APPARITIONS

With this collection, Hong Kong finally has its first magic realist. These dream-nuanced pieces splatter our senses with a veritable chiaroscuro of fanciful images, phantasmagorically tripping one over another across every page. This is no chemically-inspired jaunt, but rather the psychedelic wanderings of a craftsman inspired by Borges, by Márquez and by Allende, yet—most especially in the vast sprawl that is the titular extravaganza—[it] remains *sui generis*. The Orient and Catalonia merge seamlessly in one kaleidoscopic poetic imbroglio!

—Vaughan Rapatahana, PhD
> Poet, literary critic, essayist and novelist, winner of the inaugural Proverse Poetry Prize

Sevilla's *The Year of The Apparitions* removes barriers between life and death, creating a chiasmus of the causality and casualty of both in a liminal world that is full of returns to childhood, nostalgia for lost innocence, unforgettable sensory experiences that never completely diminish, oral and sexual desires of a carnivalesque body that seems to be there all the time in the background, smelling ethereal smells of parties, drinks and cigarettes.

The poet's distinctive voice grapples with illusive images and voices, as well as with the physicality of *the* voice itself and its limitations—the fact that it can be imprisoned. What is doubtful to Sevilla, more than those illusory images and voices, is their receiver; it is the senses of the seer and the listener that cannot be trusted—an ambrosial erosion of self at the very moment of deciphering external phenomena.

Unwilling to be fooled by ideologies yet recognizing that those same ideologies form an inescapable trap for the human subject, the poet's subjective voice seems to reflect a fundamental desire for transgression, yet shows at the same time the maddening impossibility of transgression as long as it is imprisoned within language and culture.

Sevilla's language carries an inwardness that lets signifiers sing on their own; past and present traumas unfold in between commas, overloaded words seem to be squeezed out of a grinding machine—sometimes at an amazingly speedy tempo. It is a language with an urgency to narrate experiences in a personal poetic way, yet also with an acute awareness of itself as an unreliable medium of communication; a language which knows that it creates the façade we call the world.

—Ahmed Elbeshlaw, PhD
Independent Scholar of Comparative Literature, author of the poetry collection, *Savage Charm*.

One key line in the collection *The Year of the Apparitions* is 'Rome does not pay traitors' (36)—one which is followed a little later by another which reverses that statement; 'Rome always pays traitors'. These lines puzzle, deliberately: Rome the centre of spiritual authority (for a Catholic, for a Spanish individual) and Imperial authority— needing traitors?—yet short-changing them? Rome requiring traitors and paying them? Either way, the city remains powerful, in charge, able to pay even after betrayal. Rome survives by betrayal, then. Here we see the fascination that politics has for poetry. José Manuel Sevilla dedicates his anthology of surreal images and starkly contradictory lines—some with the reality of a dream, mental translations from a first language (Spanish) to English—to 'the heroes of Catalonia and Hong Kong'. Does Rome represent Madrid in its opposition to Catalan independence? Or Beijing in relation to Hong Kong? Or, because this is the English language, the more insidious power of American culture, also felt here, over all other cultures, betraying them, not least through the power of its language? Whatever is the case, this poetry asks about survival in the face of treachery or betrayal, and if we think of survival, we may remember J.F. Lyotard's definition: A survivor is one who knows he should have died. Who survives here? Rome, whether this is Madrid, Beijing or Washington / Hollywood? Or those who stand in independence against it? Betrayal and survival are two clues here to this poetry, which expresses personal dreams, yet knows these are conditioned by the forms politics take, which produce both of them.

—Jeremy Tambling, PhD
        teaches as Professor of English at SWAP University Warsaw, and used to be Professor of Comparative Literature in Hong Kong, and Professor of Literature at Manchester before retiring.

The Year of the Apparitions firstly impresses me with its art of irony. Reading this poetry stimulates me with vivid imaginations as if I am watching a movie. The art form of irony is usually manifested through WORDS in a novel or poetry; also manifested through storytelling by actors in a movie or video. In *The Year of the Apparitions* storytelling is enabled by ironically deriding IRONY; actors may excel in a special acting technique through ironically deriding IRONY.

Secondly I read *The Year of the Apparitions* with strong resonance to realistic life experiences that are emotionally and permanently retained as memories.

Rather than using fancy words to praise *The Year of the Apparitions*, one may simply measure its truth as literature: if a collection of poems can deliver its art of irony and resonance to one's emotional memory, it is more than a successful work.

—Yang Yee Shan

Poetry books (in Spanish):
. "From the limits of paradise", 1991, Editorial Betania, Madrid
. "Alice in Ikea's Catalogue" and "The Night of Europe", 2004, Editorial Betania Madrid
. "C" by Peter Reading, translation into Spanish and prologue, La poesia señor hidalgo Editorial, Barcelona
. "Ashes of Auschwitz and Eighteen Dogs", Angel Urrutia Poetry Prize award 2009, Lekunberri, Navarra
. "Family Album", 2016, Editorial Lord Byron Madrid

Theatre:
. "El Puente", 2000-2001, Barcelona and other cities in Catalonia and Spain
. "The Bridge", 2011 McAuley Studio Theatre Hong Kong
. "Sombras, Sol y Flamenco" (Ballet by Ingrid Sera-Gilet), 2012, Sheung Wan Civic Centre, Hong Kong
. "Kennedy", 2016, McAuley Studio Theatre Hong Kong

Anthologies:
. "Trayecto contiguo", 1993, Editorial Betania Madrid.
. "Sonia Wants to Rent an Apartment", 2012, first prize of the Cha Encountering Poetry Contest, Asian Cha magazine Hong Kong
. Poems in "Otro Canto", 2013, Editorial La Pereza, Miami
. Poems "Of Words and Keys", 2018, in "Mingled Voices 2", by Proverse Hong Kong.
. Poem in "Voice and Verse", 2018, in CHA Tenth Anniversary Anthology
. Poem, 'The Talking Photo', 2019, in "Mingled Voices 3", by Proverse Hong Kong.

POETRY PUBLISHED BY PROVERSE HONG KONG IN ENGLISH

Alphabet by Andrew Simpson Guthrie

Astra and Sebastian by L.W. Illsley (*teenage epic*)

The Bliss of Bewilderment by Birgit Bunzel Linder

The Burning Lake by Jonathan Locke Hart

Celestial Promise by Hayley Ann Solomon

Chasing Light by Patricia Glinton-Meicholas

China Suite and other poems by Gillian Bickley

For The Record And Other Poems Of Hong Kong
     by Gillian Bickley

Frida Kahlo's Cry And Other Poems by Laura Solomon

Heart to Heart: Poems by Patty Ho

Home, Away, Elsewhere by Vaughan Rapatahana

The Hummingbird Sometimes Flies Backwards
     by DJ Hamilton

Immortelle and Bhandaaraa Poems
     by Lelawattee Manoo-Rahming.

In Vitro by Laura Solomon

Irreverent Poems For Pretentious People by Henrik Hoeg

The Layers Between by Celia Claase (*Collection of poems
     and essays*)

Life Lines by Shahilla Shariff

Moving House and Other Poems by Gillian Bickley

Of Leaves and Ashes by Patty Ho

José Manuel Sevilla: The Year of the Apparitions   68

Of Symbols Misused by Mary-Jane Newton

Over the Years by Gillian Bickley

Painting the Borrowed House: Poems by Kate Rogers

Perceptions by Gillian Bickley

Rain on the Pacific Coast by Elbert Siu Ping Lee

Refrain by Jason S Polley

Savage Charm by Ahmed Elbeshlawy

Shadow Play by James Norcliffe

Shadows in Deferment by Birgit Bunzel Linder

Shifting Sands by Deepa Vanjani

Sightings: a collection of Poetry by Gillian Bickley

Smoked Pearl by Akin Jeje

To Eastern Lands by Roger Uren

Unlocking by Mary-Jane Newton

Violet by Carolina Ilica

Wonder, Lust & Itchy Feet by Sally Dellow

The Year of the Apparitions by José Manuel Sevilla

INTERNATIONAL PROVERSE POETRY PRIZE ANTHOLOGIES

Mingled Voices ed Gillian and Verner Bickley

Mingled Voices 2 ed Gillian and Verner Bickley

Mingled Voices 3 ed Gillian and Verner Bickley

Mingled Voices 4 ed Gillian and Verner Bickley

POETRY IN CHINESE

Moving House and Other Poems by Gillian Bickley (in Chinese with additional contents & b/w photographs)

EDUCATIONAL
(English Language)

Poems to Enjoy, Book 1 by Verner Bickley (3rd Ed) w. 1 audio CD (Graded poetry anthology w. teaching and learning notes, glossary, etc.)

Poems to Enjoy, Book 2 by Verner Bickley (3rd Ed) w. 2 audio CDs (Graded poetry anthology w. teaching and learning notes, glossary, etc.)

Poems to Enjoy, Book 3 by Verner Bickley (3rd Ed) w. 2 audio CDs (Graded poetry anthology w. teaching and learning notes, glossary, etc.)

Poems to Enjoy, Book 4 by Verner Bickley (3rd Ed) w. 2 audio CDs (Graded poetry anthology w. teaching and learning notes, glossary, etc.)

Poems to Enjoy, Book 5 by Verner Bickley (3rd Ed) w. 3 audio CDs (Graded poetry anthology w. teaching and learning notes, glossary, etc.)

FIND OUT MORE ABOUT PROVERSE AUTHORS, BOOKS, INTERNATIONAL PRIZES, AND EVENTS

Visit our website:
http://www.proversepublishing.com
Visit our distributor's website: www.cup.cuhk.edu.hk

Follow us on Twitter
Follow news and conversation: <twitter.com/Proversebooks>
OR
Copy and paste the following to your browser window and follow the instructions:
https://twitter.com/#!/ProverseBooks

"Like" us on www.facebook.com/ProversePress
Request our free E-Newsletter
Send your request to info@proversepublishing.com.

Availability
Most books are available in Hong Kong and world-wide
from our Hong Kong based Distributor,
The Chinese University Press of Hong Kong,
The Chinese University of Hong Kong, Shatin, NT,
Hong Kong SAR, China.
Orders and enquiries: Email: cup@cuhk.edu.hk
Website: www.cup.cuhk.edu.hk

All titles are available from Proverse Hong Kong
http://www.proversepublishing.com
and the Proverse Hong Kong UK-based Distributor.

We have stock-holding retailers in Hong Kong,
Canada (Elizabeth Campbell Books),
Andorra (Llibreria La Puça, La Llibreria).
Orders can be made from bookshops
in the UK and elsewhere.

Ebooks
Most Proverse titles are available also as Ebooks.